magnesium

magnesium © 2016 Ray Buckley

Cover Photo by Cheyenne Montgomery
Edited by Laura Garwood

Published 2017 by Belides Publishing Group

Ray Buckley is an American author from Portland, OR. He is an actor and cinematographer.

ISBN 978-0-9976773-1-7

ACKNOWLEDGEMENTS

Independent Publishing Resource Center
The Domestics
Powells Books
Daniela Cosovic, Ian Stewart, & Mac Pogue

CONTENTS

magnesium

INTRODUCTION

I've attempted several times an introduction to this work and have several times failed. There's very little hope for curating what is herein contained, and I'm perhaps a fool for trying again. Just live with me for a moment as I fill out this page.

I've before referred to this work as a catalogue, which still, despite the trouble with previous iterations of this description, seems the truest out of all I can apply to it. What it is a catalogue of, is perhaps the matter in question. I can't say exactly.

I hope to charge someone else with the task of figuring that out. I don't have a doctorate, as much as I'd like one, so making examinations of texts according to academic standards is really well beyond my purview. Odd how that works.

Well. This is *magnesium*.

I wrote you a poem,
I titled it after the flower
you chose when I described
to you the method we should
employ for identification purposes.

It was meant as a thank you,
but I wasted it on one of those
moments in which I write bad
poetry. So you won't be seeing it.

Instead, I've decided to write
you another, hoping that chances
will make it that I write it
well this time.

You did many charming things,
some of which I did not witness
first hand, but you told me about.
And it endeared you to me.

I want to thank you.
For not being what probability
had high hopes of making you.

I'm not sure how to tell you this
without writing bad poetry.
You were very kind to me.
And I want to thank you.

It's so unfair of you
to stand there
with your red hair
and all of your reminders.

ONE TOO MANY THINGS

I've written one too many things that are too grave to go into this book.
I've written one too many things.

I've written one too many things that are too prophetic.
I'm under qualified for that kind of work.

I wonder often where it is I'll be filed in the ongoing records
kept by people who take it upon themselves to keep records.

I am preoccupied by this daily.
A significant percentage of my wakeful thoughts are concerned with it.

I work very hard to guarantee that I will be looked upon favorably
by the documents which catalogue the activities of the significant.

I work very hard to be considered significant.
I have intentions of having a very elevating photograph taken of me

at some point so it can accompany the paragraphs I've written
dedicated to my abiding attention to my own immortality.

I do not approve of the way you've chosen to organize our lives.
I spent years writing manifestos about my difference of opinion.

None of them survived. My wife asked me to burn them.
Unfortunately I did not act quickly enough and now she is not

My Wife.

Lizzy, I come to talk to you when I'm tired
and when other people aren't listening.

I don't know why they aren't listening,
but they're not, so listen to me.

Lizzy, just a few words tonight.
I haven't yet written anything properly

for you. Well, maybe one thing, but
only one and a sort of prologue.

I'm still trying to figure out what to
say. But tonight I don't have any

drugs. And I'd like to think
that despite what happened

I'd be in better shape to say something to you
if I had something other than 2631 in my system.

I had to pull the bottle out to
find that serial code. I'm considering

eating this tab now in honor of you.
It just seems like something you'd appreciate.

In place of all those books
on philosophy I pledged to write,
I've catalogued several
years of missing you.

Talking to oneself in the voice of Beckett makes talking to one-self an elevated form. What one should consider under these circumstances is whether one has anywhere to be. And most likely, under these circumstances, he does not.

Given fully to those things which govern the world, he is left ashamed of how small he is. Prepared to immolate him-self in the name of the Word, the God, the Mother, Gaia, Mu-hammed, Buddha, Vishnu, the Great Elk of the Sacred Forest, Lono, Capitalism, Communism, New Age Medicine, Essential Oils and the Atom.

To tear apart the products for being products is a wanton act of confused cruelty. We blame them for our identity crisis. We blame them for having convinced us, but we forget that we have made them in our image, and they are the bastard children of our reluctant work. They have endured our abuse because we hate ourselves. Release the son from the crimes of the father. Civilized law decrees it.

We hate the coffee for its ambiguous origins, which could be bloody, or could be not. There are days when the package assures us we are making great strides in human decency by going through with the transaction. Other days it will not be so generous.

The analog radio waves which were once open to the free market for one-way transmission into homes is now the sole property of the government, reserved for National Emergency. Which will release us from dullness.

A need for eternity is satisfied by the cyclical nature of the calendar. We designed it and the clock so there would be some-thing in the world which would assent to our belief in resur-rection.

Contrivance is the human attempt to emulate nature.

8

Organizing it according to a fiat is an attempt at locating God. The traffic lights are divine in this way.

Smokers congregate in the reservations which preserve their way of life in the overwhelming excess of the unstoppable modern way. Cancer rates are much higher among them. They know they are dying, and we pity them, but understand that they were never given the chance to advance as a sovereign nation.

MYSTERIOUS SALES

Feed me your secrets,
And put an end to your
Mysterious sales.

Your work is first rate.
Your product incomparable.

I received word of your
Goods when your salesman
Came to my door

And presented me with
The brochure.

Which I read at the
Bottom of a very deep
Night.

So now I'm here,
Here at your troubled kiosk.

And I ask you to feed me
Your secrets. And to put an
End to your Mysterious sales.

BACH

I've just been untruthful, unsuccessfully, to someone whom I owe full disclosure.
Though more of what she's owed is that which I feigned to be held from doing.
So everything went wrong.
And now I'm hoping these Chorales of Bach will palliate the symptoms of shame I'm now enduring.

ASSURE ME

Stay with me. Assure me of things I know I can't be assured of.
Press your will against the arguments which mortality makes
against us.

Say to me that the work I do will keep us persistent through the
years we were not allotted.

And if all we are given is this pittance,
let us feast despite our economic situation.

I think perhaps a terrible crime to commit is to fill someone's ear with garbage as they lay dying.

GOOD ART

I love tribute too much to make good art.
Holy art will humble itself before you.

I KNEW IT WAS YOU

I knew it was you who would come.
You who have adorned my body in glistening admiration.

Your work is done and it shines impressively.
Now I challenge you to find me under all this light.

Great lapses in security
have shaken me.

I grow aware of my
frivolous spending.

Though to spend frivolously
and regard it so
requires general frivolity.

So I don't know what to do.
But in any case,

this lapse in security has
me shaken.

And I don't know what to do.

On occasion, relevant concerns
will reach me from the chaos of
my wildest thoughts.

On occasion. Often it will be
that I can hope for a scant
idea or two. One worth

the attention I've been rigged
to give it.

Anyway. Now is not one of
those times.

I require a saline IV and a thorazine drip.
Please make no objections. I will be in
your debt and you will have achieved benevolence.

I'm not entirely sure what to think this evening. I've put a requirement of one page on myself, and though my expectations are low, I hope the content I fill it with will not be bile.

Anyway. I've written thus far tonight a few poems. I've recently taken it upon myself to abandon the central subject of my book. I think to avoid condemning the work to an abiding and singular preoccupation.

I've felt, I've thought, or rather I've been concerned, that so much attention to you might hurt the expression of you. That there would be no foil. Or something. Somehow I'd betray you by making you the entire breadth of it.

These are just a few thoughts. I've taken up taking narcotics again. The days have been much work, and not this work, the right kind of work, but the work which provides for my financial security. So at night, I've been retiring to chemicals.

It's very pleasing right now to be free of the stress of complete sobriety, particularly one weary from the stress of efforts I'm ambivalent to spend.

I miss you. Some nights are harder than others. Forgive me for my candid weakness, and whatever offense this commits to art, but I need you with unconscionable desperation.

I was watching some throw away television from the nineteen-nineties and the actors in the romantic relationship do a very good job performing the scripts. They have good pathos. And on a narcotic I'm inclined to remember you. And to hurt quite a lot for it.

Michael's in a relationship now. Another one. I don't know who he was with when we were together, probably no one, until Delaney, but I don't know if you really ever knew her. Besides, that didn't last long and I've heard twice Michael repudiate the relationship in its entirety; he seems to regard it as an adolescent

19

tangent. Nothing valuable. But sometimes Michael's mind crops up with a mystery like that. I don't know. Maybe he was trying to impress someone with his capacity for indifference. I don't remember who we were with.

He's in a relationship now and I'm not sure why I'm telling you this, other than the fact that we both enjoyed his company and his idea of entertainment—he's fronting a band and the press is quite generous with their praise. He's a tad rustic for my taste, but that's mostly his collaborator's doing, who sings, writes, and plays a lot like someone from rural Oregon. It's odd. But both have punk sensibilities which make up for their pastoral leanings.

He's well. I'd like to take you to one of his shows, just because that's something we used to do and I think you'd enjoy it. Well, at least, I think you'd enjoy the act of doing it; perhaps not the details so much, but the atmosphere and, preferably, most notably the company. This would certainly be the case with me. All the event would be secondary, but Michael's usually a good time, and I'd enjoy the digression so long as we'd accompany each other.

Remember the bathroom at the Hangar show? I sometimes forget how audacious we were in combination. Like what we did in the park in virtually wide open space in perfect view of all those houses and the people walking the concrete path.

I love you. There's not much for me to do but resign to the desire to say it. I'm often far too direct to satisfy the expectations of art.

So, let me transgress one more time.

I love you.

UNTITLED

I'm sorry Ray. I'm sorry I can't speak to you. I'm sorry that there's nothing I can say to you ever again. I'm sorry we'll never know each other. Little attempts over the years are clear we can't. Little failures to add to the rest.

My daughter's eyes are not your eyes. I did not give her the name we chose. She was conceived in your absence and in your absence everything happened.

UNTITLED

When truly you knew how tired I was, it came to you you had to leave.

Too much the weight of those burdens I hastened to carry, too much and too high those judgements I labored to calculate. That road of thought I undertook to tread was too dim under untrustworthy light.

You went back to the world and you were right to go back. Thank you for the time you spent with me and thank you for being so gentle.

I have intentions of departing
not long after everyone wakes up.
And as early as etiquette allows.

It would make things easier
if I had any control over this
thing I spend my time doing.

I CANNOT BE YOURS

I cannot be yours.
To be yours is to be taken from the world, he said.
His eyes were magnificent with high resolve, and higher cure.
Fierce and exotic thoughts ran wild through his mind.
He knew things no other man had known.
He was sick with a sickness no other body had host.

His spirit was wild, and barely contained by his body.
At times it stretched out, where the pressure of physical form
gave way to sheer unnatural will.

She of Earth reached out.
Her limbs were fire and she made her commandments.
Her will clapped like thunder and shook the world.

But spirits not of body do not obey the laws of physical things.

Her will which is the mountains, and her need which are the
deepest parts of the ocean, are the remains of sadness left in
the world.

JOHN CASSAVETES' A WOMAN UNDER THE INFLUENCE

What can I say? There's nothing to be said. You feel aged about forty years, you look twenty, no one takes you seriously. They say if you were born a hundred years ago you'd make sense. But right now you're just a curiosity at best and you know that with that kind of praise you're without it the worst kind of pariah. You don't know where to take yourself, or in which world you might feel welcome, let alone which you're actually welcome in set aside the way you feel.

Your writing is shot, because it was bad to begin with and it got worse with time and nothing you do you feel was worth doing and nothing you feel you can ever do. You're overcome by sloth, and often times the words you choose you find indicate you're a person you're not. Sometimes they take you for, well you're not sure what they take you for but you can be quite certain from the look in their eyes it's not who you feel is resident the host.

Let it go. Stop wishing for all those things which are now memories and memories only and but a bit of content for your fantasies in the late evening when you're wide awake to the sound of your life.

An immense cool factor came with insomnia in high school but that time is long over, and now there's just the pain of sleeplessness, which feels a lot like a terminal illness, or watching John Cassavetes' *A Woman Under The Influence*.

I'm growing anxious to leave
though most everyone must be present
before I do if I'm going to
satisfy etiquette.

EVERYTHING

When you moved to the city and took up residence
on Alberta you were under the impression that
this would change everything.

Your new house with its charming cornices
and molding is not fit to release you from
your obligations to fate.

You owe it more than you can take out in loans
in the form of house shows and gatherings.
The courts will see to it that you pay the merchant.

People who care too much are a stale attraction.
Pick up your avarice. Look away from your awe.
It's unbecoming of an artist in the modern era.
Our eyes are too open to endure how appalled
you are at everything.

A BRANCHLET OF STAR MAGNOLIA

Let me leave for you a brief something to honor our time together.
A terrible wilderness of lives is where we made contact.
You left your loneliness on the shelves of bookstores.
And wondered about melancholy.
It's because of you I have any regard for the forest.

He wore a mask.
And behind it he kept secrets.
He wrote a book.
And bled into it a thousand regrets.

And although the pages were illegible,
everything it suggested was enough
to maintain us.

THE DEFINITION OF THE WORD GRACE

I remembered what the word grace meant, looking at you.
I had no idea how wrong all the world was;
their fashion sense,
their preferences.

You wear better shoes than they do.
You put your hair up better.
And when it's down, it's down
better than I've ever seen it on anyone.

I miss your clothes,
the baby doll dresses,
the colors you took from the Earth.
Your utter royalty.
Your natural tendency to outdo everyone.

This hunch I'm earning is not
worth the discomfort it costs.

—Get up.
—I don't want to go anywhere.
—Please?
—No.
—Please?
—Where do you want to go?
—Anywhere! Just wake up!
—Okay.
—Yes!

I ran out of narcotics. But I have this bottle of muscle relaxers.

It's very good for one's career to affect a drug problem.

Do not take your own picture.
Stop doing this.
Let others take your picture for you.
You will feel better the next day.

—I was not prepared.
—I know you weren't.
—I was not immune.
—I know.
—I was just as vulnerable.
—I know you were.
—You had higher responsibilities.
—Don't say it like that.
—That's how you would have said it.
—I know.
—The weight is too much now.
—I know.
—I took care of you once. You held me and I held you. I was not immune. I would have taken care of you.
—I know. But it's the weight of it all,
—And I couldn't cure it. I was at your bedside and still sickness was all you could talk about. You loved being ill more than you loved me.
—Don't say that.
—And you imagined better medicine.
—
—And I wasn't it.
—
—I was vulnerable.
—
—And you left me every fever. You were gone when you surrendered to the pleasure of illness.
—
—And my promise to bind myself to you as each wave overtook us
—Stop.
—was not enough. You had ambitions of conquering the ocean.

THE RULES OF THIS GAME

I had forgotten the rules of this game.
Forgive me for thinking I had a say.
These things are very confusing you know.
Provide me time in which to learn.

This pupil of yours is weak and human.
He will put his regard for himself
back in the becoming place.
And defer to your Wisdom.

It's very good for one's lover to give a kiss now and again.

I was mistaken when I said
those things to you.

I'm apologizing now.
For being wrong and for
being very sure I wasn't.

PSALMS

I read the myths of our people,
and they were thoroughly dissatisfying.
They didn't include you.
They didn't dedicate a page, a verse,
or even a tiny Psalm.

I undertook to rewrite them.
I'm not finished yet
but I can tell they'll be much better.

The romantics make their
return to the world of pop music
and pop music derides them for
their adherence to the old
outdated ways.

I abandoned the pact we made.
I went to bed with every person
in the world.
They thanked me.
I told them it was only right.
They took to congratulating me.
And it was then I realized
I had abandoned the pact we made.

I've made the mistake today of yielding to the
admonitions of the commercial which asserts
that all I need to avoid the danger is to
make the purchase.

I made the purchase.

I could not elect you immune from death.
Despite my ambition.

So if death takes, I will
dispossess us of everything.

And so grant us immortality.

Send me away to a prison where they keep magicians.
So I can perform my magic for those who are in on the secret.

VERSE WILL HOPEFULLY FORGIVE MY UNWARRANTED HARSHNESS

Laura, I'm writing this for you.
Who knows if you'll read poetry
or if you read poetry,
but there are things that need to be said.

You have to be careful with the one
who's given himself carelessly to your
company. I imagine proximity is all
that is needed for all those wrong things

to happen that will no doubt go wrong and happen.
You're lovely, so know that I understand.
You're quite stunning, in an arresting way,
but I know you made a big fuss

about how when the crowd called for everyone to turn
and kiss the closest stranger, he demurred
like the breed your kind is trying to kill.
This is why you need to be gentle.

So if you read poetry,
do me a favor and remember fragility
and remember that this is not such a bad thing to be.

I remember when we used to mutilate ourselves.
And how beautiful the act was.
Now I see scars on the arms of women.
And I can barely contain myself.

I saw him recently.
We all remember him well,
but if you can avoid it,
try not to see him again.

Her years leading up to her twenty-first birthday were counted out by a riding crop against her thighs as she bent over for J R during the filming of her contractual obligations. During the drive home she described them as an affirmation of self and an act of pride. Which I didn't dispute.

Over crepes she informed me of the work she had lined up and I told her it was her choice who she undressed herself for and she smiled at me.

May I sing a prayer for you?
May I ask your permission?
May I need you?
Will it be alright if we forget
for a moment the autonomy
modern wisdom has sold us on?
May I be powerless for a moment?
Will that be alright?
May I?
May I be powerless?

FOR LIZZY

Alright, before I retire to
tonight's narcotic,
I want to say a few things
to you Lizzy.

A MINOR DIGRESSION

Allow me for a moment to remove myself
from my most pressing contemporary occupations.
Which have advanced toward the very personal.
For the moment, let me return to the old concerns,
which had some thought on making corrections.

For the senators, are you aware that it is not your
job to have an opinion? Do you understand the
intended function of your occupation?

A politician takes great care with tact.
This is his obligation.
He is diplomatic in all matters.
He is gentle, he is subtle, he is careful.

Members of government, you have misplaced yourselves.
Those who want great for a particular outcome
are not the appropriate managers of state.

The appropriate managers of state are indifferent.
They will work according to the needs of those
who petition them.

Forgive me for being so heavy-handed,
though perhaps it's necessary.
I would not have ever thought it necessary.
But you have convinced me that we must regress
to those most elementary of lessons.

The government is not the people.
The people should not be governing.
They will act according to their petty interests.

A politician, whom I've said,
takes great care with everything,
should do so according to the wishes of the population,
and use his skill as diplomat to play arbiter and dispel the
natural tendency to disorganize back to violence and usurpation.
And protect our fragile constructive attitudes.
If you have wishes, senator, you have taken the wrong course in life.

That is all.
I will return to the present.

AND WE ARE UNDER IT

This is a body barely alive.
Do you understand that?
He is kept in grace only by
the expressed will of sky.

And it's then that I wish I hadn't
thought otherwise.

And left to acquire you eternal life.

BE GRACE

Be grace, idol of wisdom.
Dream deity of the final run.
Whose light shimmers like infinite wisdom.
And whose eternity shines like eternity.

Reveal yourself from your gowns of air.
Which wrap you in invisibility.
And give you vast access
to the dreams which are dreamed by the Earth.

And all her children.
They are awake in the idea of you.
Wondering when their life
will open like your wisdom opened

at the beginning of everything.
And left in it a sense of longing
for things your radiation suggest.
Love me with your forever love.

Open again on this spot of air
I have chosen for you.
Come to me in all your allness.
Bring all what you bring.

Come onto these shores
like you were in a boat
and carrying a parcel
for all our dreams to see.

Wonder for us.
Give us ideas like the ones
you bade us to have
when you started it all.

Tell us how you started it all.
Grow roots in us which we'll
wish ourselves the prisoners of.
Reach in like all there is is reaching.

Be grace, and tell us your secret.
Like eternity, shine like eternity.
Go into us, contain us.
And be grace.

Harper Lee and many other books
were the subject of conversation last night.
Though reluctant, I engaged them on this topic.

—You can never write a novel.
—I can never write a novel?
—No. You're not capable.
—Why am I not capable?
—Everything's too magnificent for you. You won't be able to let go of that.
—That will hinder my ability to? To wh—
—You're going to want to write the bible and no one is going to want to read the bible.
—Because?
—Because no one cares. They're not interested in the new revelation—the new knowledge. They want a reflection of themselves, they're not curious about your insights and they're not curious about your reverence. The first is irrelevant to them, and the second is sickening to them.
—I'm too—
—You're too—
—Too what?
—You're very—
—I'm too sentimental?
—No you're—well yeah, but—
—I'm too? otherworldly?
—No that's not it.
—I really want to know.
—You're just. I don't know where any of it comes from. Like, what does any of it matter?
—None of it matters.
—Basically.
—I'm too concerned with things that don't matter.
—Yes.

—What should I do?
—Start caring about other things.

—Do you understand there is absolutely no relevance to anything you can possibly put together?

—Yeah.

—Are you sure? Because from the look of this desk you're still trying.

—Well, yeah, I guess—

—There's no hope for you. Look at this.

Picks up a piece of paper.

—Look at this.

Reads.

—*Whose eternity shines like eternity?* Are you serious?

—Yeah, I guess—

—This is ridiculous. *Whose eternity shines like eternity?* What century are you living in?

—Does it—

—And this one.

—I don't want to hear about all the women you praise.
—I don't know why I consider you a friend.
—You don't have a lot of options.
—No. I don't.
—You'll get used to it.

DR. WHITAKER

He opened the world. And where it opened he decided what the weather should be. But the skies were disobedient and did not change.

There are countless things I am too overcome by to speak of coherently and evenly. There are pages and pages concerned with these topics, but they are incomprehensible. Some I will include in this book. Others I will keep removed.

One of these concerns a woman I spent a great deal of time with. Her work was to alarm me out of my skin. She wore clothes that suggested poetry and lived in apartments that suggested culture. She smoked very deftly and looked very qualified doing it. She talked a lot about coffee.

When I grew to be a bore, she called me to inform me she was leaving me for her coworker who looked suspiciously similar to David Foster Wallace.

When he grew to be a bore, and I moved into an apartment which suggested culture, and began to wear clothes that suggested effort, and learned how to brew coffee, she asked me if I would take her back. She said the coffee was really good.

I'm so envious of you. I'm motivated more than most things by envy. I admire so many people. And I want to be everything you are.

Did I make you believe I didn't want you?

Was I so consumed by servitude that you began to believe it was deception?

That maybe, I wanted someone else?

And when you discovered my remorse for an old tragedy, you mistook my grief for the thing that could explain it all.

Here you knew, I could not love you.

Is that what happened?

I've only recently come to understand this possibility. I didn't know why you were so angry. I couldn't consider what you were considering. The fact of my loving you was too true in my mind to permit thoughts to the contrary. I loved you. I wanted you. All those outlandish explanations were truth. I really thought myself the property of the world. And I thought I could not hold you.

I'm sorry I made you believe I was a liar. The strangeness of my honesty was a red herring.

Do you remember when I toured you through those documents when you asked to see all my secrets? I did it to dispel your fear. It wasn't for torture.

I had no idea apology could look so much like affair.

You wrote their recipient some December in the future to assure her that all you ever wanted from this narrator was his friendship. I don't know how to properly explain to you how false everything you believe is.

You abdicated. This was the exit your eternal grace could permit. You put down your coronet. You gave him up to whom you thought was the one. You read abandonment in those lines. You read he was never yours. And your pride is too great for a thing like that.

FOR LIZZY II

Alright Lizzy,
I've just taken that narcotic.
I'm several minutes away from any
effect, but perhaps now is as
good a time as any to begin.

There are words you have said
and things you have done
which have reached me through
the press that have drawn you
my dearest compassion.

Whatever happens, I just
want you to know—you have
a friend.

And I'll set fire to the journalists
on your behalf if at a moment
you're feeling like violent
retribution is the right course.

If not, I'll simply be prepared
to carry out any wishes, whims,
or desires you may find yourself
at any moment overtaken by.

LOATHING AND SELF HATRED

I thought there was freedom in this line of work but I was wrong.
I put undue faith in the lines I constructed.
And really, what use is there in telling you anything?

I seriously doubt there's anything I can write of interest to you.
You who've chosen for no reason I can conceive to read these pages.
Or perhaps just this page.

My best work is an impression.
I would think, though I could be wrong, in which case
my best work is actually someone else's.
I'm angry you weren't at the show this evening.

You didn't know it was happening, but you should have been there
by some serendipitous circumstance and I'm holding it against you
that you weren't. You should have imposed on me.
You would have been received very well.

The religious books you have written are a mistake. You have fallen into awe and you will confuse everyone with your attitude which is neither devout nor secular. Go back to your revolutions. Revelation doesn't want you. Go back to your stars and your flags. They want you. You make a good soldier. You do not make a good prophet.

Sarah Blasko sang to me in a hotel lobby.
I wanted to release myself to the sea like
she implored.

She advertised all this freedom, and I
needed every ounce of it.

Breathe deeply. Sing holy notes which are silence. Wish again for the pantheon you have nothing to do with. Try again to cure her of the mortal illness. Wish away the debt every man is born with and expected to pay. Take out your loans in argument against the sky. Tell him everything that is not enough is enough and he's a fool to refuse you.

Administer your cure. Your empty syringe. Your dust. Your cold air. Time has folded itself away from you. And you wish that wishes had the power hands believe themselves to possess.

Time like moments you now only remember.

So much time gone by and

She died.
I looked at the water.
I looked at the landscape.
It came to me how unaware it was. Just there.
So thoroughly unaffected.

Tis a shame. That so attractive a man be beaten to an extent that it would damage his beauty. You'd expect something more of him, something gregarious and loud, something to join in at the party. But something comes over him so. Something dark strange, absent of all the alluring mystery you'd otherwise expect it to have. He is charm incarnate. The only in flesh. He is a quavering shell of a man. With pain and ugliness deep beneath his loveliness.

WHAT DO YOU THINK OF IT?

What do you think to be so large in my mind and seven years away?
I have praised you.
I have put you in books.
I have given you wishes.
I have put you on stage.
I have said your name in unconscious mantra.
Is this my need for religion, dissatisfied by religion?
What do you think of it?
Do you know that it's merely the most obvious thing?
Can you understand that?

I am overcome with hate for the moments that don't include you.
Those are many.
I am overcome with hate for the labor that goes into art.
I'm tired of art.
There's too much art.
Art is the poorest substitute.

The maintenance of my survival is worth very little.
This is a conditional proposition.
What do you think of it?

Sometimes famous singers sing to me
and they sing to me about all those things
I did to you which were completely wrong.

YOU ARE THE MYSTIC

You are the mystic.
Immune to analysis.
You are the prophet born to a world
built on math instead of miracles.

Incantations come to you in sleep,
and leave you with the faint impression
that all your expectations
went unmet.

I RECALL A MANMADE APERTURE

I recall a, most likely, manmade
aperture in the forest wherein
you wed your fiancé.

I recall friends, gathered around
fine baroque furniture and stacks
of comfortable pillows.

I remember strangers, too young
for us to invite to our group
without connotation.

I recall a particular set of
circumstances involving me
which were questionable.

Then there were other things,
less significant, like friendly
exchanges initiated.

These were talks brief and
amicable, laughing, and
career motivated.

We were all much closer
that evening than we had
previously enjoyed.

Broken pairs, taboos, and
confusion were partial
contributors to our

Sudden and inexplicable
closeness. Certain careful
men among us had lost

Their fathers. Others had
made dire mistakes of
attire.

OUTDATED FRUSTRATION

What have you done?
You put your hand down to rest
and in doing so condemned us all.

It's your fault we age.
You've done it to all of us.

You are the cornerstone of delusion.
You are like the First Thursdays
And the Minden Mondays.

You are all those events which delude us into
beliefs such as are endemic of youth.

Put yourself back to work and remember.
Stop having children.
Stop gathering around bon fires.
It's legal now, you can no longer do it illicitly.

I really like your tattoo.

When you moved to the city and took up residence
on Alberta you were under the impression that
this would change everything.

Your new house with its charming cornices
and molding is not fit to release you from
your obligations to fate.

You owe it more than you can take out in loans
in the form of house shows and gatherings and
whatever new designation you have for party.

You are the refrain of a very terrible and interminable song.

Who will be Manson this time?
Who will be Baez?
Who has come to play us their songs?
Who will reveal us to what we are thinking?
I'm going mad with the knowledge that
despite the fact that this is now a platitude,
we're repeating ourselves.
Are you listening?
Why do you go according to the wishes
had for you by every generation that came before?
Even your repudiation of it is an exact replica of
their activities.

Now's not a time for poetry.
Now is a time for mourning.

For mourning my limp leg.
And resenting the crutches.

After writing this it became apparent to me that Beckett wrote many of his plays on very little sleep.

VOICE

VOICE. Good morning. I say that to the morning. Witnesses. I have them. In the form of your ears. Eyes. I'm your orator. Welcome to the morning. Here in the morning with me. I've come a long way through the night to meet you in the morning. Do you understand?
ANOTHER VOICE. No. I don't. I don't understand.
V. No. Why would you. You. Living here. Born according to my will nothing more than a voice in the morning.
A. What makes you speak?
V. Yes.
A. Who am I?
V. Nothing.
A. I am nothing.
V. Nothing. A voice that I meet in the morning. I've been awake with my fear and I've done nothing. Years of nothing.
A. You shake your head. In disapproval.
V. If I have even the will.
A. To disapprove?
V. To disapprove with so much energy. With so much emphasis.
A. Shaking your fist at?
V. Her.
A. Her.
V. Yes.
A. Her.
V. Yes.
A. For leaving?
V. Yes.

A. Why?

V. I left.

A. So she left.

V. Yes.

A. You shake your fist at her?

V. If I have the energy. For so much emphasis.

A. You disapprove?

V. If I have the energy.

A. Of whom do you disapprove?

V. The time.

A. Does it change the answer?

V. Yes.

A. It's morning.

V. It's morning.

A. Yes. Who's listening?

V. You are.

A. I am.

V. Yes. You asked me.

A. I asked you. I asked you who has your disapproval.

V. Yes.

A. You didn't answer.

V. I would have answered.

A. No.

V. You're right.

A. You're right.

V. Is there time? Gather me away. Give me what I've asked for.

A. You can't have them.

V. I know.

A. I know.

V. Give them to me.

A. They're not mine to give.

V. You're a voice in the morning.

A. Yes.

V. Yes.

A. Do you understand?

V. Yes.

A. I can't give it to you.

V. Why.

A. It's not mine to give.

V. I want it.
A. I know.
V. I know.
A. I know.
V. Give it to me.
A. I can't.
V. Where is she?
A. She's gone.
V. Where did she go?
A.
V. Where did she—
A. What time is it?
V. It's morning.
A.
V. It's morning.
A. Morning.
V. Yes.
A.
V. Where is she?
A. Gone.
V. Gone where?
A. Gone away.
V. Away why?
A. Why?
V. So I would be alone.
A. Why?
V. So I could be with her.
A. Why?
V. In her loneliness.
A. Yes.
V.
A. Gone.
V. She's gone.
A. Yes.
V. Gone.

V. What time is it?
A. It's morning.
V. Yes.

A. Yes. It's morning.
V. Yes.
A. What is it like in the morning?
V. It comes very quickly.

PICCADILLY CIRCUS

Two men approach a phone booth advertising credit card acceptance.
A. Yeah, card.
They enter the phone booth.
A. Well, the cool thing about, well, okay. Um. Okay, it takes,
B. I don't have my card.
A. Do you have the number?
B. What? Oh.
A. I have it.

A. It's good to be in a small place that smells like piss with you.
   Let's see.
B. Which number is it?
A. It's this one right here.

A. Okay. So where are we?
B. Um, Piccadilly Circus.
A. And we'll be next to the fountain with the, no that's—
B. She'll know what that is.
A. Yeah but it's too,
B. What?
A. We should be like right outside Ripley's Believe It or Not.
B. Cool. Well uh, that has like,
A. Multiple entrances?
B. Yeah, no the fountain's a good idea. Let's do the fountain.
A. But, but that's like, it's bigger...
B. How about the island? The island. The island in the center. It's
near the fountain. It's just like, the sidewalk stop. It's like in the
middle of the street.
A. No that's not, that's not concise enough.
B. Why's that not concise enough?
A. How bout we'll be right outside the Sting.

B. Where's the Sting?

A. It's that building, do you see the, you probably can't see the sign. You have glasses on, see the Sting?

B. Is it the tiny thing above the awning?

A. Yeah.

B. Yeah. Let's do the Sting.

A. Or right outside the thing that says, that's advertising thirty-nine steps. You see that?

B. Yeah I do.

A. The sting? Is it the Sting?

B. How about, how about Crown Gift. Crown Gift. That looks good. That's not going to be anywhere else. Or is that not open enough?

A. Yeah but it's not like, I want it to be closer to the circle.

B. Okay, yeah, then the Sting. The Sting is the best.

A begins dialing the phone. He pulls a credit card from his pocket and an accidental ten pound note.

A. Fucking currency in this city.

A swipes the card.

B. I think that's the wrong orientation.

PHONE. (*chime*) we're sorry...

BABYLON

Babylon has come again to do its work on us.
The kind we're all aware of.

And I don't understand you any longer
and the myth hasn't helped explain.

When alive in the palm of a god one can't afford to consider he may not be there.

Here are the laws. Three pages. Three pages before morning. Or I will elect myself inept and irrelevant. A terrible fever overtook me last night. (It's morning already, the sun rose suddenly against my attention which had lapsed.) And I was desperate to find a passage from a book I wish someone else hadn't written, for a beautiful description that I had intentions of appropriating.

This didn't work out however. I was in a pained fever, wishing I had your body. Wishing I weren't alone on this frameless basement bed. I am sick with need. I am need. Bring me something that will alleviate a rush and a fever. Remove me from this suffering which is now of the body and not just of the heart—who has reluctantly borne the duties that man imposed on him which have nothing to do with blood. Poor scientific thing, burdened with mystical responsibilities.

This long without departure has made me ill with the illness which is a violent attack on idleness to take some urgently needed, but ambiguous action. I'm furious with confusion and ineffable insatiable angst. And it's collecting prodigiously and unforgivingly at a high temperature in my previously saintly and monk-pure idol of a body.

I want to taste your thighs. And I will not care about things like plagiary. Let me rest against your heat. And be kissed by the waters of your swollen and beautiful flower.

The heat and the fever are terrible afflictions on the night. In it I can never sleep, and now I cannot sleep and now I cannot sleep and now I cannot sleep and Which is a violent reminder of my loneliness in the world. Which grows quite more obvious as I continue on, making my way through sunrise, wishing I'd fall into the hypnosis which I'm being held violently (and unwillingly) on the threshold of.

The laws. Return to the laws. Grant them religious status

and harvest from them your work. Which is rumored and quite possibly fraudulent.

The temperature of the air around you is falling. And you're now feeling animosity toward your fever for leaving you. But you can't call it up again or you'll be tempted to remove it. And you suspect that all will be gone from you if you don't

What?

Perhaps there are places you can go to find love but even the old neighbor girl who trotted back in, whom is tortured by your inability to unfix your gaze from Her, is gone because you cannot unfix your gaze from Her.

Grant me repose. Allow me drink from your Eternal Water. Remove me from the confusion death pain of the threshold. These are things I wish. These are wishes which are in your offices to Grant or Deny. What is it like to be deity? What is it like to have split in two? To be of Earth and of Sky and command Oceans and produce warm like you were the rainforest?

These are black pages bought with a great deal of strategy. I will forget everything and so look for nothing. I will empty the sky of its promises and swallow them. I will accept the refuse as acceptable. Only if it comes with eternity. Which I've decided is an Unfair price, but if all sales are final, then bring me the product I've chosen, which is pantheon.

And goodbye Lady who is fire in me and in all things. And remember what I did which was refuse you for rumors of a very high place.

I am thief. I am parlor trick. I am parakeet. I am echo I am reverberate. I am illness. I am loss. I am what one thinks of himself as he looks in the proud mirror. I am captain. I am dock. I am the idea that the idea had regarding important things.

You are Anne Sexton.
She is Dorothy Parker.

You have been to Bedlam.
And she probably has enough rope.

Look, I don't have much strength.
Not right now, please.
Let's talk for a while.
Alright.

Rachel, hello, how are you? I've had
you on my mind of late. You've

drifted in from your warehouse in
London. Which has been fitted

to house you and your friends.
My vulgar American life has left

me wishing I could be in your
London. Speaking with you and

your dissident artist friends.
Who have so many bad things

to say about the aristocracy, like
we say bad things about our

child president and his cabinet.
But your disapproval is so much

lovelier than mine. I wish I could
hate the aristocracy.

FOR YOUR REVIEW

I wonder sometimes,
and often,

I'm wondering about something
that requires far more discipline and far
more endurance than I personally possess.
So I wonder, but not very well.

Then I begin to pace. And I think about
other things I've thought about recently.

But I can't remember them very well.
And then a conversation starts.

You set your hands to a task that can't be completed.
You lost track of time, you forgot my name.

I left you to your work. I had that child we talked about
having. Sometimes she asks about people like you.

What do you think I should say?

YOUR INSTRUCTIONS

Can you remember a few things for me?
Thank you. You're very kind to come to my assistance.
This is what I need.
Take these items and carry them with you.
As you carry them, I want you to do that
remembering we talked about.

This is what you'll remember:

INDEX OF TITLES

CPSIA information can be obtained
at www.ICGtesting.com
Printed in the USA
BVOW06s1416180118
505543BV00031B/3/P